Fun Fan Facts:
The Unofficial NBA Edition

Utah Jazz

Everything Young Utah Jazz Fans Should Know

By: Jake Liam

Dedication

To every Jazz fan who has explained, at least once, why a team in Utah is called the Jazz.

This one is for you, the Stockton believers, the Malone loyalists, and anyone who still gets a little quiet when someone brings up the 1998 Finals. You know what happened. We all know what happened. We just do not talk about it.

And to Salt Lake City, the most basketball-obsessed city that no one ever suspects is basketball-obsessed. Keep surprising people.

THE NBA BY THE NUMBERS

MOST NBA CHAMPIONSHIPS*

- CELTICS (18) †
- LAKERS (17)
- WARRIORS (7)
- BULLS (6)
- SPURS (5)

As of the 2024-25 Season. † One Trophy = 4 Championships.

NBA HISTORY SNAPSHOT

- **1946** NBA Founded
- **1954** Shot Clock Introduced
- **1979** 3-Point Line Added
- **2023** NBA Cup Introduced

BIG NUMBERS

$156 million
Stephen Curry's est. earnings in the 24-25 season

7'7"
Tallest player in NBA history (Gheorghe Mureşan & Manute Bol)

30 | 4 | 82

- **30** Teams Competing in the NBA
- **4** Playoff Rounds
- **82** Games Per Season

UTAH JAZZ
IN THE NBA

- FOUNDED: 1974 †
- NBA TITLES: 0
- CONFERENCE TITLES: 2*

32 Playoff Appearances

*† Founding dates are complicated & may cause arguments at Thanksgiving. Ask someone born before color TV. All Titles reflect pre-relocation franchise history. * As of 2024-25 Season.*

NBA ALL-TIME MVP LEADERS

KAREEM ABDUL-JABBAR (6) ★ MICHAEL JORDAN (5) ★ BILL RUSSELL (5)

EASTERN CONFERENCE

- Atlantic – **Celtics**
- Atlantic – **Nets**
- Atlantic – **Knicks**
- Atlantic – **76ers**
- Atlantic – **Raptors**
- Central – **Bulls**
- Central – **Cavaliers**
- Central – **Pistons**
- Central – **Pacers**
- Central – **Bucks**
- Southeast – **Hawks**
- Southeast – **Hornets**
- Southeast – **Heat**
- Southeast – **Magic**
- Southeast – **Wizards**

WESTERN CONFERENCE

- Pacific – **Lakers**
- Pacific – **Clippers**
- Pacific – **Warriors**
- Pacific – **Suns**
- Pacific – **Kings**
- Northwest – **Nuggets**
- Northwest – **Timberwolves**
- Northwest – **Thunder**
- Northwest – **Trail Blazers**
- Northwest – **Jazz**
- Southwest – **Mavericks**
- Southwest – **Rockets**
- Southwest – **Spurs**
- Southwest – **Pelicans**
- Southwest – **Grizzlies**

Introduction

Welcome, fans! Whether you're new to cheering for the Utah Jazz or you've been bleeding the team colors your whole life, this book is packed with fun, exciting facts about your favorite team. Get ready to impress your friends and family with everything you know about the Utah Jazz.

Quick Timeout

This book is packed with stats. Like, A LOT of stats. Every fact was checked, double-checked, and triple-checked. But here's the thing about basketball history: not everyone agrees on everything. Ask someone who watched games before color TV and someone who grew up with instant replay and you'll get two completely different answers. My dad, stepdad, uncle, and grandpa all argued about the same fact. Four people. Four answers. All of them think they're right. So if you spot something that doesn't match what you've heard, congratulations. You might be a bigger fan than the people who helped make this book. And honestly? That's pretty cool.

HOW IT WORKS

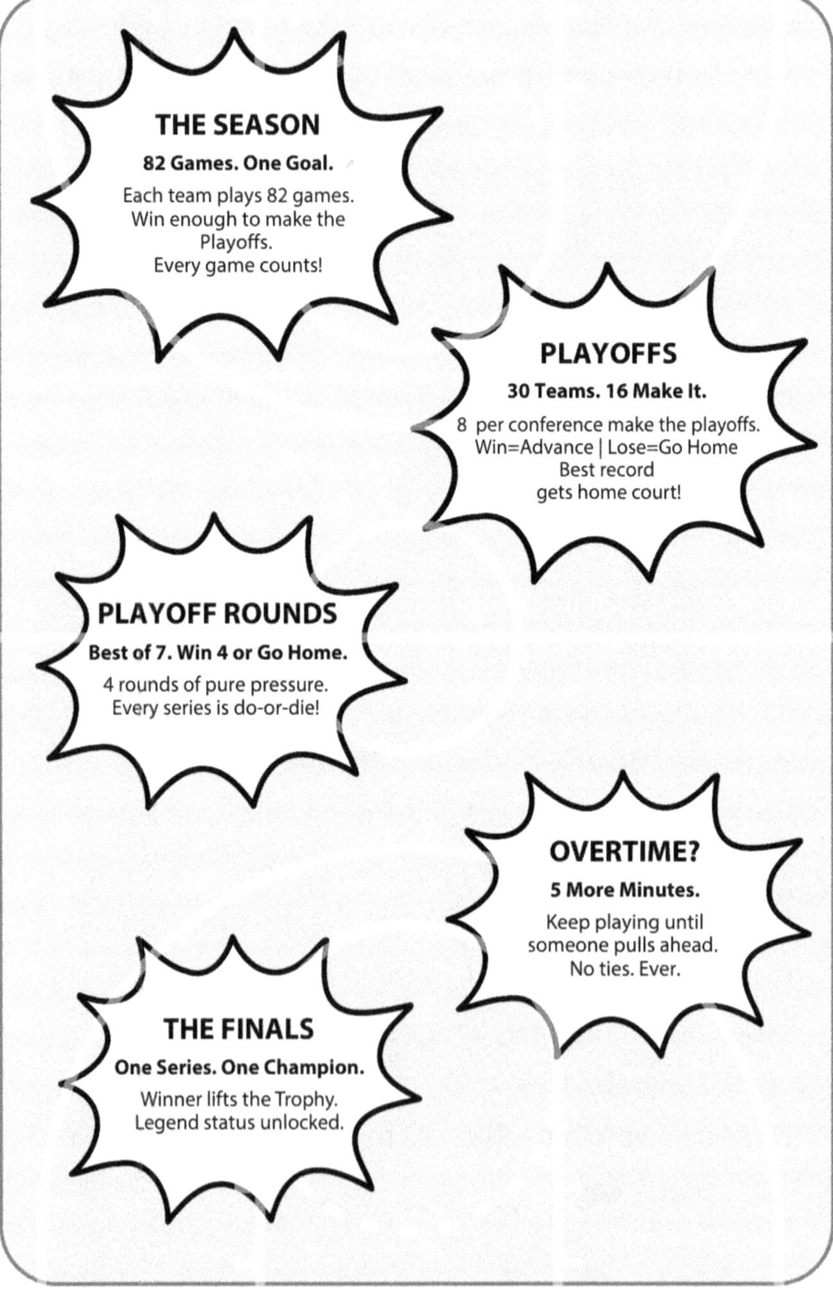
THE SEASON
82 Games. One Goal.
Each team plays 82 games.
Win enough to make the
Playoffs.
Every game counts!

PLAYOFFS
30 Teams. 16 Make It.
8 per conference make the playoffs.
Win=Advance | Lose=Go Home
Best record
gets home court!

PLAYOFF ROUNDS
Best of 7. Win 4 or Go Home.
4 rounds of pure pressure.
Every series is do-or-die!

OVERTIME?
5 More Minutes.
Keep playing until
someone pulls ahead.
No ties. Ever.

THE FINALS
One Series. One Champion.
Winner lifts the Trophy.
Legend status unlocked.

How the NBA Works

At first glance, basketball feels simple. Ten players. One ball. Two hoops. Go.

Then the NBA adds the layers.

An 82-game regular season. A draft where bad teams pick first. Playoffs that last two full months. Superstars who can change everything with one trade. Dynasties that rise, fall, and rise again.

And somehow, it all works.

The NBA is built on one big idea: every team gets a chance to reset, reload, and rise again. No relegation. No dropping down to a lower league. Just basketball, every night, from October through June.

It is a league designed for drama, stars, and comebacks. And once you understand the flow, it is impossible to stop watching.

The League Setup

The NBA has 30 teams, spread across the United States and Canada. Those teams are split into two conferences:

- Eastern Conference
- Western Conference

Each conference has three divisions, mostly based on geography. Divisions matter for scheduling, but not as much as they used to.

Every team plays 82 regular season games, usually from October through April. Home games. Road games. Back-to-back nights. Long road trips. The season is a marathon before the sprint even starts.

Win games, and you climb the standings. Lose too many, and the pressure builds fast.

How Games Are Played

An NBA game has four quarters, each lasting 12 minutes. That means 48 minutes of game time, plus timeouts, free throws, and the occasional coach argument that adds another 20 minutes nobody planned for.

Scoring is simple:

- A shot inside the three-point line is worth 2 points
- A shot beyond the arc is worth 3 points
- Free throws are worth 1 point

If the score is tied at the end of regulation, the game goes to overtime, which lasts 5 minutes. Still tied? Another overtime. Keep going until someone wins.

There is a shot clock too. Teams have 24 seconds to take a shot. No standing around. No holding the ball forever. Keep it moving.

The Regular Season Race

The regular season is long for a reason. It tests everything.

Depth. Health. Focus. Patience.

Teams play opponents from both conferences, but they face conference rivals more often. By the end of the season, each conference's top teams have earned their playoff spots the hard way.

The goal is simple: make the playoffs. But there is a twist.

The NBA Cup

In 2023, the NBA added something new to the middle of the season. Something with actual stakes. They called it the In-Season Tournament, now known as the NBA Cup.

It works like this: Every team plays a small group stage during November and December, with special court designs that look like nothing else in basketball. The best teams advance to a knockout round held in Las Vegas.

The winners split a prize pool. Players earn bonus money. And for the first time, a team could lift a trophy before the playoffs even started.

Some fans are still warming up to it. Some players love it. But the moment a team starts treating it seriously and a crowd shows up buzzing in December, it feels like something.

Which, honestly, sounds about right.

The Play-In Tournament

Instead of sending the top eight teams from each conference straight to the playoffs, the NBA added something new. The Play-In Tournament.

Here is how it works:

- Teams ranked 1 through 6 in each conference are safe
- Teams ranked 7 through 10 fight for the final two playoff spots

The 7 and 8 seeds have an advantage. Win once and you are in. Lose and you still get one more shot. The 9 and 10 seeds have to win twice in a row just to earn a first-round matchup.

It turns the end of the season into a sprint. Every game suddenly matters more. Fans love it. Coaches age rapidly.

The NBA Playoffs

Once the playoffs begin, everything tightens.

Sixteen teams enter. Eight from each conference. Every round is a best-of-seven games series. That means the first team to win four games moves on:

- First Round
- Conference Semifinals
- Conference Finals
- NBA Finals

Home-court advantage matters. Crowds get louder. Rotations get shorter. Superstars play heavier minutes. One bad quarter can flip a series. One great performance can define a career.

By the time the NBA Finals arrive in June, only two teams are left. One from the East. One from the West. Four wins away from a championship. Four wins away from history.

The NBA Draft: Hope Begins Here

Here is where the NBA gets clever. Every summer, new players enter the league through the NBA Draft. Teams take turns selecting college players, international stars, and teenagers straight out of high school.

The teams that finished with the worst records get the best odds to pick early through the Draft Lottery. It is not guaranteed, but it gives struggling franchises a real shot at changing their future with one pick.

That means one bad season does not doom you forever. It might actually change everything. Some franchises are rebuilt by a single draft night moment.

Hope shows up wearing a new jersey.

No Relegation. All Pressure.

Unlike many global sports leagues, NBA teams never drop down to a lower league. They always stay in the NBA.

That does not mean there is no pressure.

Fans remember losing seasons. Owners make changes. Coaches get replaced. Players get traded. Every year is a test of direction, patience, and belief.

Stars, Systems, and Showtime

The NBA is famous for its stars. But stars do not win alone.

Teams need chemistry. Coaches need systems. Role players need to deliver on the biggest stages. One injury. One hot streak. One trade deadline deal. Any of it can flip a season.

That balance between individual brilliance and team basketball is what makes the league special.

Fast breaks. Buzzer-beaters. Game 7s. And moments that get replayed forever. That is the NBA.

Once you get the flow, it is pure electricity.

Utah Jazz Facts

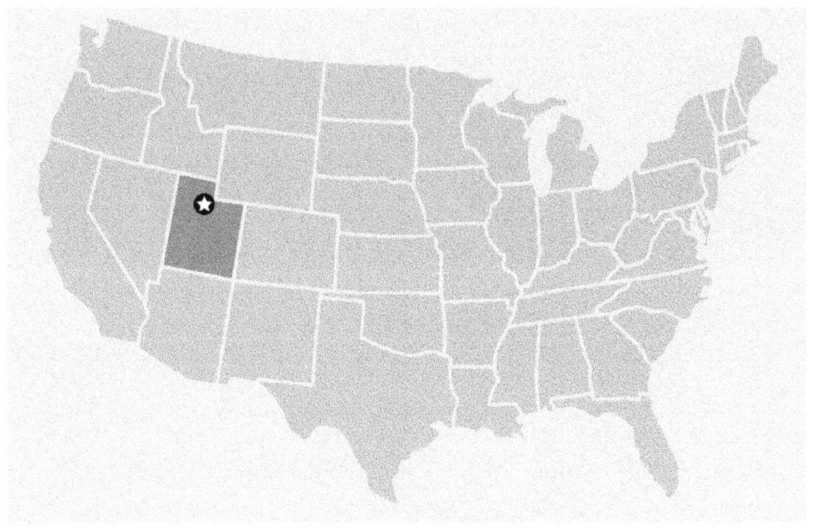

Home City

Salt Lake City, Utah

Metro Area Population

About 1.2 Million

Home Arena

Delta Center

Arena Capacity

18,306

Conference / Division

Western Conference / Northwest Division

Famous Local Food

Fry sauce, funeral potatoes, fry bread, Crown Burger

Chapter 1: From New Orleans to the Mountains

1. Born in the Big Easy

The Utah Jazz did not start in Utah. Not even close.

The franchise was born in New Orleans, Louisiana, in 1974, and if you know anything about New Orleans, you already understand the name. New Orleans is the birthplace of jazz music. It is a city built on brass bands, second lines, and music floating out of every door on every street. Naming a basketball team the Jazz there made complete, perfect sense. It was like naming a Boston team the Lobsters, or a Chicago team the Deep Dish. It just fit.

The NBA was expanding in the early 1970s, adding new cities and new franchises, and New Orleans got one. The Jazz played their first season in 1974-75 at the Municipal Auditorium, then moved to the Superdome, which was so enormous it sometimes felt like watching basketball inside an airport. The crowds were enthusiastic, the city loved having a team, and for a few years, it actually worked. Then things got complicated, rosters got thin, and the money started running out.

But before any of that, they had one player who made the whole city stop and stare.

2. Why "Jazz" in Utah?

Here is the question every Utah Jazz fan has been asked at least once: why is a team in Utah called the Jazz?

Utah is not exactly known for jazz music. Salt Lake City does not have a French Quarter. There are no brass bands parading down Main Street on Sunday mornings. Jazz as a genre and Utah as a state have roughly zero historical connection. And yet, when the franchise packed up and moved from New Orleans in 1979, they kept the name. The new owners considered changing it. Fans debated it. And then everyone just kind of shrugged and moved on.

The reasoning, such as it was, came down to practicality and brand continuity. The team already had jerseys, merchandise, and a growing fanbase. Starting over with a new name meant starting over with everything. So the Jazz stayed the Jazz, even in a state where the most popular music might generously be described as not jazz. Today it is one of the NBA's most recognizable quirks, the kind of thing that gets brought up in sports trivia nights worldwide. Imagine you move from the most musically rich city in America to the mountains of Utah and just decide to keep rolling with it. That is a level of commitment that deserves some respect.

3. Pistol Pete: The Wizard of New Orleans

Before Karl Malone. Before John Stockton. Before any of the greatness Utah fans would eventually claim as their own, there was Pete Maravich, and he was something else entirely.

Pete Maravich, nicknamed Pistol Pete, was one of the most creative basketball players who ever lived. He dribbled behind his back before that was normal. He threw passes that seemed physically impossible. He scored from angles that made coaches cover their eyes. In the 1976-77 season, Maravich averaged 31.1 points per game for the Jazz, which led the entire NBA. He was putting up video game numbers before video games existed.

Maravich grew up practically attached to a basketball. His father, Press Maravich, was a college coach, and Pete spent his entire childhood in gyms, inventing moves and practicing tricks that nobody had seen before. By the time he reached the pros, he was already a legend. His time with the Jazz in New Orleans was the peak of his career, a dazzling, almost surreal stretch of basketball that had fans packing the arena just to see what he would do next. He played the first 17 games of the 1979-80 season in Utah before being traded to the Boston Celtics.

4. The Big Move

By the late 1970s, the New Orleans Jazz were in trouble.

Attendance was dropping. The team was not winning enough. The city loved its Jazz, but love does not pay the bills, and the bills were piling up. The ownership group was struggling financially, and the NBA was not in a position to bail anyone out. Something had to change. In 1979, that something turned out to be everything. The franchise relocated to Salt Lake City, Utah, becoming one of the most unlikely transplants in professional sports history.

Salt Lake City was smaller than New Orleans. Much smaller. It was not a city with a long professional sports history, and nobody was entirely sure how basketball would land there. The answer turned out to be: extraordinarily well. Utah fans adopted the Jazz immediately and ferociously. The team found a home in the Salt Palace arena, and even through the early losing seasons, the community showed up. There is something about a smaller market getting a major league team that creates a different kind of loyalty. Salt Lake City did not take the Jazz for granted. They had almost not gotten them at all, and they never forgot it.

5. Finding Their Footing (And a Guy Named Stockton)

The first few years in Utah were not pretty.

The Jazz spent the early 1980s figuring out who they were, churning through rosters, and finishing near the bottom of the Western Conference. They had flashes of promise and stretches of frustration, the standard experience of a young franchise still searching for its identity. Then the 1984 NBA Draft happened, and everything changed, quietly, without much fanfare, in the way the best things in sports sometimes do.

With the 16th pick, the Jazz selected a guard from Gonzaga University named John Stockton. Stockton was not a flashy prospect. He was not the most athletic player in the draft. He was undersized, came from a mid-major school, and did not look like a future Hall of Famer from the outside. Nobody paid much attention to pick number 16 that day. The record books would eventually have a lot to say about that. So will Chapter 2.

Two years later, in 1985, the Jazz used the 13th pick on a power forward from Louisiana Tech named Karl Malone. Again, solid pick, no fireworks. No one in the building could have known that they had just drafted the engine of one of the greatest partnerships in NBA history. Sometimes the best stories start with no one paying attention.

6. Karl Malone: The Mailman (1985-2003)

There is a reason they called him the Mailman. Karl Malone delivered. Every single night, in every single game, for eighteen seasons in Utah, he showed up and did exactly what power forwards are supposed to do, except better than almost anyone who ever played the position.

Malone came out of Louisiana Tech in 1985, built like he had been constructed in a laboratory rather than born in a small town in Louisiana. He was not just strong. He was legendarily strong, the kind of player who made opponents quietly reconsider their career choices before tip-off. His work ethic was famous around the league. He lifted weights obsessively, ran in the offseason when everyone else was resting, and treated his body like a professional obligation. The result was a player who remained dominant well into his late thirties, which in NBA years is basically ancient.

Over his career with the Jazz, Malone won two MVP awards, made fourteen All-Star teams, and scored more points than almost anyone who has ever played professional basketball. He finished as one of the highest scorers in NBA history, a number that stands as a monument to consistency more than flash. He never had a signature move that ended up in a shoe commercial. What he had was relentless excellence, game after game, year after year, for nearly two decades. The Mailman always delivered. That was never really up for debate.

7. John Stockton: The Point God from Gonzaga (1984-2003)

John Stockton does not look like the greatest point guard in NBA history. That is actually part of what made him so dangerous.

He was not the biggest guard on the floor. He was not the fastest. He wore shorts that, by modern standards, would be considered disturbingly small. He did not have a signature celebration or a nickname that required explanation. He was from Gonzaga University in Spokane, Washington, a school that was not yet the basketball powerhouse it would later become. He was quiet, almost aggressively ordinary in his presentation, the kind of player who looked like he should be teaching gym class rather than dismantling NBA defenses.

What he actually did was become the most precise, reliable, and devastatingly consistent point guard the sport has ever produced. Nineteen seasons. Every single one in Utah. He never asked out, never demanded a trade, never chased a ring somewhere else. He just showed up, ran the offense, and made everyone around him better with a calm that bordered on unsettling. He ran the Jazz offense with the precision of someone who had memorized every possible outcome before the ball was even inbounded. Imagine an air traffic controller who also happens to be unstoppable with a basketball in his hands. That was John Stockton, every night, for two decades.

He ended his career with a record that deserves its own fact and gets one. When you read it, you will understand why nobody is ever catching him.

John Stockton scans the court with the calm focus that made him legendary. Quick passes. Perfect timing. Stockton led the Utah Jazz for nearly two decades and still holds the NBA records for assists and steals. The Jazz reached the NBA Finals in 1997 and 1998, but fell just short of the title against Michael Jordan's Chicago Bulls. *Photo: John Stockton (1988-89). Photograph via Wikimedia Commons. Licensed under CC BY-SA 3.0. Source: Wikimedia Commons.*

8. Adrian Dantley: The Forgotten Scoring Machine (1979-1986)

Before the Mailman. Before the Point God. Before any of the Jazz's greatest era, there was Adrian Dantley, and if you only know Utah Jazz history from the Stockton-Malone years, you have been missing something important.

Dantley arrived in Utah when the team relocated from New Orleans in 1979, and he immediately became the best player on the roster by a considerable margin. He was a forward with an almost supernatural ability to get to the free throw line, draw contact, and convert from anywhere in the paint. He was not tall for his position. He did not overpower opponents athletically. What he had was footwork, intelligence, and a relentless determination to put the ball in the basket by any means available. He won two NBA scoring titles during his career, both coming in the years he spent putting the Jazz on his back before the franchise found its long-term cornerstones.

Dantley made six All-Star teams over the course of his career and was eventually inducted into the Basketball Hall of Fame in 2008, which is when a lot of casual fans finally caught up to what Jazz historians already knew.

He was the bridge between the New Orleans years and the Stockton-Malone dynasty, the player who kept Utah competitive and showed the city what professional basketball at its best could look like. He never got a dynasty. He never got a Finals run. But he gave Utah something to believe in during the years when belief was in short supply.

9. Donovan Mitchell: Spida (2017-2022)

Donovan Mitchell came to Utah wearing a Spider-Man backpack to his introductory press conference. That should tell you everything you need to know about his energy.

Mitchell was drafted 13th overall in 2017, which is the kind of selection that generates mild excitement rather than headlines. The Jazz liked him. The analysts thought he had potential. Nobody quite predicted that within one season he would be finishing second in Rookie of the Year voting and single-handedly dragging the Jazz into must-watch playoff basketball. He earned the nickname Spida partly from his love of the Marvel character and partly because his game had that same quality: patient, precise, and then suddenly everywhere at once when you least expected it.

His five seasons in Utah were filled with highlights, playoff heroics, and the kind of big-moment performances that turn players into legends. He put up 57 points in a playoff game against the Denver Nuggets in 2020, one of the greatest individual playoff performances in recent memory. He made multiple All-Star appearances and became the face of a franchise that had not had a genuine star to build around since the Malone and Stockton era. When the Jazz traded him to the Cleveland Cavaliers in 2022, it marked the end of a chapter and the beginning of a rebuild. Utah got a remarkable collection of draft picks and young players in return. But Spida left a Spider-Man shaped hole in the Delta Center that the city still feels.

10. Lauri Markkanen: The Blue Flame (2022-present)

Nobody saw Lauri Markkanen coming. That is not an insult. That is genuinely one of the best things about his story.

Markkanen came to Utah as part of the trade that sent Donovan Mitchell to Cleveland, which meant he arrived in a city still processing the departure of its most beloved player in years. He was a 25-year-old Finnish forward who had shown flashes of brilliance in Chicago and Cleveland but had never quite put a full season together. Jazz fans were intrigued but cautious. The rebuild was just beginning, the expectations were being carefully managed, and Markkanen was one of several pieces arriving at once rather than a centerpiece of anything.

Then the 2022-23 season happened. Markkanen averaged over 25 points and nearly nine rebounds per game, shot beautifully from three-point range, and played with a confidence and consistency that nobody had quite seen from him before. He won the NBA's Most Improved Player award for that season, which sounds like a quiet honor until you realize what he actually improved from and to. He went from promising but inconsistent to one of the most effective forwards in the Western Conference, almost overnight. He became the kind of player Utah fans show up early to watch warm up. The rebuild suddenly had a face, and it belonged to a quiet guy from Finland who just needed the right home to become something special.

Chapter 3: So Close, So Many Times

11. The Pick-and-Roll: The Play That Broke the NBA

The pick-and-roll is not a complicated play. That is the whole point, and also the cruelest part of it.

Here is how it works. One player sets a screen, which means they stand very still and let a defender crash into them. The ball handler uses that screen to get free, and then the screener rolls toward the basket looking for a pass. It has been part of basketball forever. Every team runs it. Every coach teaches it on day one. It is, on paper, about as threatening as a knock-knock joke. And then Stockton and Malone ran it, and suddenly every defense in the NBA started having nightmares about something they had seen a thousand times before.

What made their version different was repetition turned into perfection. They ran the pick-and-roll so many times, in so many games, over so many seasons, that it stopped being a play and became more like a natural disaster. You knew it was coming. Everyone knew it was coming. The other team's coaches knew it was coming, the fans knew it was coming, probably the hot dog vendors knew it was coming. It did not matter.

Stockton would find Malone cutting to the basket with the kind of accuracy that made other point guards stare into the middle distance and quietly question their life choices. Opponents game-planned against it for years and still could not stop it. That is not a basketball play. That is a magic trick that works even when you know exactly how it is done.

12. The 1997 NBA Finals: Utah's First Dance

In 1997, the Utah Jazz did something the franchise had never done before. They made the NBA Finals. The city of Salt Lake City essentially lost its mind in the best possible way.

The Jazz had spent years building toward this. Stockton and Malone were in their prime. Jerry Sloan had the team playing the tightest, most disciplined basketball in the Western Conference. They stormed through the playoffs with a confidence that felt different from previous seasons, like the team finally believed what everyone watching them had believed for years. Utah was ready. The question was whether anyone could be ready for what was waiting on the other side of the bracket.

That other side was the Chicago Bulls. Michael Jordan, Scottie Pippen, Dennis Rodman, Phil Jackson, the triangle offense, and roughly six years of accumulated invincibility. Imagine training your whole life for a swimming race and then showing up to find out your opponent is a dolphin. The Jazz competed hard. They genuinely pushed the series. Malone was extraordinary. Stockton was Stockton. But the Bulls won the championship in six games, and Utah flew home with a silver medal feeling and a burning question that would carry them all the way into the following season: what if we get one more shot?

13. The 1998 Finals: The One That Still Hurts

They got one more shot. It went about as well as Jazz fans would prefer not to remember.

The 1998 NBA Finals was a rematch. Utah versus Chicago, the same two teams, the same stakes, and this time the Jazz had the added motivation of a year spent thinking about what went wrong. They took it to six games again. The series was tighter, more physical, the kind of playoff basketball that makes you forget to breathe. Going into the final moments of Game 6, with the Jazz trailing by one point, Karl Malone caught the ball in the post with a chance to either score or draw a foul and essentially seal Utah's first championship.

What happened next became one of the most replayed moments in NBA history. Michael Jordan came from behind and stripped the ball cleanly from Malone. Then Jordan walked the ball up the floor with the clock winding down, crossed over the defender guarding him, and hit a jumper that gave Chicago the lead with 5.2 seconds left. Utah could not answer. The Bulls won their sixth championship of the decade. Jordan retired shortly after. And somewhere in Salt Lake City, a generation of Jazz fans learned that some losses do not fade with time. They just become part of who you are. The 1998 Finals is not a sore subject in Utah. It is a sacred wound, which is a completely different thing and somehow much worse.

14. Two MVPs and Zero Rings: The Malone Paradox

Karl Malone won the NBA's Most Valuable Player award in 1997 and again in 1999. Two MVPs. Fourteen All-Star appearances. One of the greatest scoring careers in basketball history. And zero championships. The universe has a strange sense of humor and Karl Malone has heard every joke about it.

The 1997 MVP was the one that stung the most for people outside Utah, because the popular argument at the time was that Michael Jordan had a better season and deserved the award. Jordan fans, which in 1997 accounted for roughly half the planet, were not shy about sharing this opinion. Loudly. Repeatedly. Across every available media format. Whether Malone deserved it or Jordan should have won it is one of those sports debates that has no correct answer and approximately one million very confident wrong ones.

What is not debatable is what Malone produced. He was relentlessly, punishingly excellent for nearly two decades. He scored 36,928 points over his career, a number so large it barely feels real. He played with the discipline and physicality of someone who genuinely believed every single regular season game carried the weight of a playoff elimination. Some players show up when the lights are brightest. Malone showed up every Tuesday night in November against a team going nowhere, and he played like his reputation depended on it. Because he believed it did. You do not win two MVP awards by accident. You win them by making basketball look like your full-time job, your hobby, and your entire personality all at once.

15. The Number That Lives Forever: 15,806

John Stockton finished his NBA career with 15,806 assists. The second player on the all-time list has around 10,000. Read that again slowly and let it settle.

That gap is not a gap. It is a canyon. It is the kind of statistical separation that makes you wonder if everyone else was playing a slightly different sport. Stockton spent nineteen seasons methodically, almost cheerfully, threading passes through impossible windows to teammates who were not yet open until suddenly, magically, they were. He did it against every defense the NBA threw at him. He did it when teams specifically game-planned to stop him. He did it so consistently that the record stopped feeling like an achievement and started feeling like a law of nature.

His assist total is the kind of number that gets more impressive the longer you stare at it. Fifteen thousand, eight hundred and six times, John Stockton delivered a pass that directly led to a basket. If you watched one of those assists per day, it would take you over 43 years to get through them all. By which point there would almost certainly not be a new leader, because nobody is catching this number. Imagine This: a record so far ahead of everything else that it does not live in the record books so much as hover above them. Every point guard who has ever done the math has quietly put the pencil down and walked away. The Stockton number does not inspire challengers. It inspires acceptance.

Chapter 4: Bears, Coaches, Traditions, and Wonderfully Weird Jazz Facts

16. Jerry Sloan: The Coach Who Never Blinked

Jerry Sloan coached the Utah Jazz for 23 seasons. Twenty-three. That is not a coaching tenure. That is a geological era.

To put that in perspective, during Sloan's time on the Utah bench, nine different people held the office of President of the United States. The internet was invented. DVDs came and went. Multiple entire music genres were born, became popular, and became embarrassing. Through all of it, Jerry Sloan stood on the sideline in Salt Lake City wearing the same expression he always wore, which can best be described as deeply unimpressed with everything happening around him. He was an Indiana farm kid who played hard-nosed defense in the NBA during the 1960s and 70s, and he brought every ounce of that toughness into his coaching career. His standards were not high. They were vertical.

Sloan demanded the same things from every player, every season, no exceptions. Run the offense. Play defense. Do not complain about playing time where he could hear you. He was old-school in the best possible way, the kind of coach who made modern players briefly consider whether their grandparents had a point about everything. He won over 1,000 games with the Jazz, guided the franchise through its two Finals runs, and earned the respect of everyone who ever played for him, including several who needed a cooling-off period first. He was inducted into the Basketball Hall of Fame in 2009, which was well-deserved and at least a decade overdue.

17. Jazz Bear: The Mascot Who Answers to Nobody

Jazz Bear is not just a mascot. Jazz Bear is a lifestyle.

He arrived on the scene in 1994, a large brown bear in a Jazz uniform who immediately set about establishing himself as the most chaotic presence in the building on any given night. His job description, on paper, involves entertaining the crowd during timeouts and getting fans fired up between plays. His actual job, in practice, involves riding motorcycles onto the court, performing dunks off trampolines, and occasionally doing things that make the arena staff quietly cover their eyes and hope for the best. He is unpredictable in the way that only someone in a giant bear suit can be, because consequences feel different when you are wearing a full costume and the whole crowd is cheering regardless.

Jazz Bear has been voted one of the best mascots in the NBA multiple times, which is a real award that real people vote on, and he wins it regularly because he genuinely earns it. He does not just stand near the team logo and wave. He commits. He trains. He apparently does enough physical preparation that his dunks are legitimately impressive, which raises several questions about the life choices that lead a person to that particular athletic specialty. Imagine you are a visiting player trying to focus on a crucial fourth-quarter possession, and a six-foot bear just did a backflip off a trampoline eight feet away from you. Jazz Bear does not care about your focus. Jazz Bear has a job to do.

18. The Delta Center: Where Road Teams Go to Suffer

The Delta Center opened in 1991 and immediately became one of the most uncomfortable places in the NBA to be an opposing player. This was not an accident.

Utah fans are loud in a very specific way. They are not loud like a city that expects to win everything and gets angry when it does not. They are loud like a place that knows exactly how good it has it and refuses to take a single home game for granted. Salt Lake City is not a sprawling metropolis with twelve other entertainment options competing for attention on a Tuesday night. When the Jazz play, the Jazz are the event. The whole city locks in, and the Delta Center fills up with the kind of noise that visiting teams mention in postgame interviews with a slightly haunted look in their eyes.

The altitude helps too. Salt Lake City sits at over 4,200 feet above sea level, which does not sound dramatic until you are a visiting player who has spent the past week at sea level trying to run an NBA offense and suddenly your lungs are filing a formal complaint. It is a small advantage but a real one, the kind of thing home teams never bring up and visiting teams always remember. The Jazz have historically been one of the NBA's elite home teams, winning at a rate that transforms their arena into something closer to a fortress. Road teams go in knowing they have to be better than their best just to have a chance, and sometimes that knowledge alone does the damage before the opening tip.

19. The Name Nobody Changed (And Now Everyone Loves)

At some point in the mid-1980s, somebody in the Utah Jazz organization presumably sat down and thought seriously about whether to change the team name. They looked at the city. They looked at the landscape. They thought about the mountains, the red rock canyons, the salt flats, and the complete absence of anything resembling a jazz club within reasonable driving distance. And then they decided to keep it anyway.

The name has been a running joke and a point of perverse pride for Utah fans ever since. Other teams have names that make obvious geographical sense. The Denver Nuggets, gold mining. The Dallas Cowboys, well, cowboys. The Utah Jazz, a music genre invented in New Orleans that has approximately no connection to the state of Utah historically, culturally, or atmospherically. And yet the Jazz did not change it, and now the name has become so inseparable from the franchise that changing it would feel like erasing something essential.

What happened, over decades, is that the name stopped being something Utah had to apologize for and became something Utah owned completely.

Merchandise sells. The logo evolved. The color schemes changed and improved. The word Jazz stopped meaning New Orleans and started meaning Stockton, Malone, Bear, mountains, and a fanbase that will pack an arena on a weeknight in January. Some names grow into a team. The Jazz grew into their name by ignoring everything that did not fit and making everything else work harder. At this point, calling them anything else would just feel wrong.

20. Fifty Years of Wonderfully Weird Jazz Facts

The Utah Jazz have been around long enough to accumulate some genuinely strange trivia, and it would be a shame not to celebrate all of it.

The Jazz have the unusual distinction of having their franchise's all-time leading scorer, Karl Malone, also be one of the top three all-time scorers in NBA history overall. That means Utah, a small-market team that has never won a championship, produced one of the two or three greatest scoring careers the sport has ever seen. Most franchises would trade their entire history for that. Utah got it and still sometimes feels underappreciated for it, which is also very on-brand.

John Stockton played 19 seasons and somehow appeared in 1,504 games, missing only 22 games across his entire career. He played through screens, charges, elbows, and everything else that comes with nearly two decades of professional basketball, and he almost never sat out. His durability was so extreme that it started to feel suspicious in the best way, like he had quietly discovered something about health and recovery that he was not sharing with the rest of the league. The Jazz also once had the NBA's best record during the regular season in 1997, finishing with 64 wins, which would be a defining achievement for almost any franchise. For Utah it remains a footnote to a Finals run that ended in heartbreak, which tells you everything about the standards this organization has held itself to since the day Stockton and Malone decided to stay together and build something worth remembering.

Chapter 5: The Reset, the Rebuild, and What Comes Next

21. The Trade That Changed Everything

In September 2022, the Utah Jazz traded Donovan Mitchell to the Cleveland Cavaliers. In return, Utah received a package of players including Lauri Markkanen. It was one of the most significant trades in recent NBA history, not because of what Utah gave up, but because of what they were building toward.

At the time, Jazz fans had complicated feelings about it, which is the diplomatic way of saying a significant portion of them were not thrilled. Mitchell had been the face of the franchise, the player who filled the Stockton-Malone sized hole in the city's basketball heart, and watching him go to Cleveland in exchange for picks and prospects required a certain kind of faith in a plan that had not fully revealed itself yet. Front offices ask fans to trust the process fairly often. Fans comply with varying degrees of enthusiasm.

What made this trade different was that Utah's front office, led by Danny Ainge, was not blowing things up randomly. They were making a calculated decision that

the team as constructed could not realistically compete
for a championship, and that the smarter move was to
collect assets, accumulate young talent, and build
something sustainable rather than chase a ceiling that
probably was not high enough. Whether that logic
holds depends entirely on how the next few years
develop. But the haul of picks gave Utah flexibility that
most rebuilding teams can only dream about, and the
young players who arrived alongside those picks turned
out to be considerably more interesting than anyone
initially expected.

22. Walker Kessler: The Human Shot Rejector

Walker Kessler blocks shots the way most people
breathe. Frequently, automatically, and apparently
without much effort.

Kessler arrived in Utah in the summer of 2022 as part of
the trade that sent Rudy Gobert to the Minnesota
Timberwolves. He was 20 years old, seven feet two
inches tall, and possessed of a defensive instinct that
made opposing players visibly reconsider their
approach to the basket the moment he entered the
game. In his rookie season he averaged 2.3 blocks per
game across 74 appearances, establishing himself

immediately as one of the most promising young rim protectors in the league. He made the All-Rookie First Team and quietly became the most exciting thing happening on a rebuilding roster.

What makes Kessler genuinely exciting is not just the blocks, impressive as they are. It is the timing and the intelligence behind them. Blocking shots at the NBA level requires reading the play, staying out of foul trouble, and resisting the temptation to go for everything and foul out trying. Kessler does all of that with a composure that most veterans take years to develop. He also catches lobs, sets screens, and runs the floor, making him useful on both ends rather than just a defensive specialist you hide on offense. Utah did not know exactly what they were getting when they traded Gobert. What they got was one of the most promising young centers in the league, arriving quietly and immediately making the building better.

23. Keyonte George: Something to Prove

Keyonte George was drafted 16th overall by the Jazz in 2023, and from the moment he arrived, it was clear he had absolutely no intention of being low-key about it.

George is a guard with a scoring instinct that seems to operate independently from the rest of what is happening around him. He can create his own shot, get to the line, and make difficult pull-up jumpers with a confidence that young players usually have to earn over several seasons before displaying it quite so openly. His rookie year had the highs and lows that most teenage NBA players experience, which is the polite way of noting that being 19 years old and playing 30-plus minutes in the NBA is genuinely hard, and nobody should be surprised when it looks hard. What mattered was the flashes.

The flashes were real and they were frequent. Games where George took over in the second half and reminded everyone watching that this was not just a project player filling minutes on a rebuilding team. This was a legitimate offensive talent who happened to be developing in public, which is how rebuilds work when they are going correctly. Utah is betting that the player George is becoming is significantly better than the player he already is, which is a reasonable bet when the player he already is can go for 30 points on a Tuesday night against a playoff team. The only question is how fast the rest of his game catches up to that scoring instinct, and all the evidence so far suggests the answer is pretty fast.

24. Utah's Basketball Culture: The Small Market That Refuses to Act Like One

Salt Lake City has a metropolitan population of roughly 1.2 million people. For context, that makes it one of the smaller NBA markets in the league. By the logic that governs most professional sports, Utah should be a place where free agents politely decline, rosters cycle through players who could not quite get a deal somewhere bigger, and the franchise exists primarily to lose respectably to teams with more glamour and more money.

Utah did not get that memo, and at this point has clearly stopped checking its messages.

The Jazz have made the playoffs consistently during the Stockton-Malone era since the mid-1980s. They have had one of the most loyal, loud, and knowledgeable fanbases in professional basketball for four straight decades. They developed two Hall of Famers simultaneously, sustained one of the great coaching tenures in NBA history, and competed for championships in the hardest era the league has ever produced. They did all of this without Hollywood, without a major media market, and without the kind of free agent magnetism that comes from being a destination city. What they had instead was organizational stability, smart drafting, player development, and a fanbase that genuinely showed up every single night and made the Delta Center feel like it mattered. It turned out that was enough, and then some.

25. Utah's Next Chapter

The Utah Jazz are in the middle of something, and the whole NBA is watching to see how it ends.

The rebuild is real, the assets are significant, and the young players arriving in Salt Lake City are generating the kind of attention that rebuilding teams rarely produce this early in the process. Walker Kessler is already one of the better defensive centers in the league. Keyonte George is developing into a genuine offensive weapon. The draft picks accumulated in the Mitchell trade give Utah options that most franchises would take a decade to collect. The front office has a plan, the ownership is committed, and the fanbase, remarkably, has remained engaged through the transition rather than drifting toward something shinier.

What Utah is building toward is a return to genuine contention, the kind of team that makes other franchises uncomfortable in April and May. It will not happen overnight, and nobody in the organization is pretending otherwise. Rebuilds done correctly take time, patience, and the willingness to resist the temptation to shortcut the process by trading away the future for a present that is not quite good enough anyway. The Jazz have been here before. They assembled Stockton and Malone quietly, piece by piece, until one day the rest of the league looked up and realized Utah had built something extraordinary. The pieces are arriving again. The mountain is patient. And somewhere in Salt Lake City, Jazz fans who have been waiting through a long rebuild are starting to feel something familiar stirring. It feels a lot like the beginning of something worth watching.

Bonus Trivia Quiz!

You think you are a true Utah Jazz fan? Try this bonus quiz!

1. The Utah Jazz originally played in which city before moving to Salt Lake City?

A) Memphis

B) New Orleans

C) Houston

D) Kansas City

2. Why was the team named the Jazz?

A) The owner loved jazz music

B) The team had a jazz band perform at games

C) The city of New Orleans is the birthplace of jazz music

D) A fan contest voted for the name

3. Which player earned the nickname "Pistol Pete" and led the NBA in scoring in 1976-77?

A) Adrian Dantley

B) Moses Malone

C) Pete Maravich

D) Gail Goodrich

4. What year did the Jazz relocate from New Orleans to Salt Lake City?

A) 1975

B) 1977

C) 1979

D) 1982

5. With which pick in the 1984 NBA Draft did Utah select John Stockton?

A) 2nd

B) 8th

C) 12th

D) 16th

6. What was Karl Malone's famous nickname?

A) The Deliveryman

B) The Mailman

C) The Package

D) The Postmaster

7. How many MVP awards did Karl Malone win during his career?

A) One

B) Two

C) Three

D) None

8. Adrian Dantley was inducted into the Basketball Hall of Fame in which year?

A) 2001

B) 2004

C) 2008

D) 2012

9. What was Donovan Mitchell's nickname?

A) Spider

B) Flash

C) Spida

D) Cobra

10. How many points did Donovan Mitchell score in his 2020 playoff game against the Denver Nuggets?

A) 45

B) 50

C) 57

D) 62

11. Which team did the Utah Jazz face in both the 1997 and 1998 NBA Finals?

A) Los Angeles Lakers

B) San Antonio Spurs

C) Seattle SuperSonics

D) Chicago Bulls

12. How many career assists did John Stockton finish with?

A) 12,091

B) 13,422

C) 15,806

D) 14,500

13. How many seasons did Jerry Sloan coach the Utah Jazz?

A) 15

B) 19

C) 21

D) 23

14. What year did the Delta Center open?

A) 1988

B) 1991

C) 1994

D) 1997

15. Which award did Lauri Markkanen win after the 2022-23 season?

A) Defensive Player of the Year

B) Most Improved Player

C) Sixth Man of the Year

D) Most Valuable Player

Super Fan Secret Challenge

Only a true Utah Jazz fan will know this.

(No Answer Provided)

John Stockton holds the all-time NBA assists record with 15,806. But how many total career steals did he finish with, making him the all-time leader in that category too?

A) 2,310
B) 2,684
C) 3,026
D) 3,265

Answer Key

1. B) New Orleans

2. C) The city of New Orleans is the birthplace of jazz music

3. C) Pete Maravich

4. C) 1979

5. D) 16th

6. B) The Mailman

7. B) Two

8. C) 2008

9. C) Spida

10. C) 57

11. D) Chicago Bulls

12. C) 15,806

13. D) 23

14. B) 1991

15. B) Most Improved Player

NBA PLAYOFF BRACKET

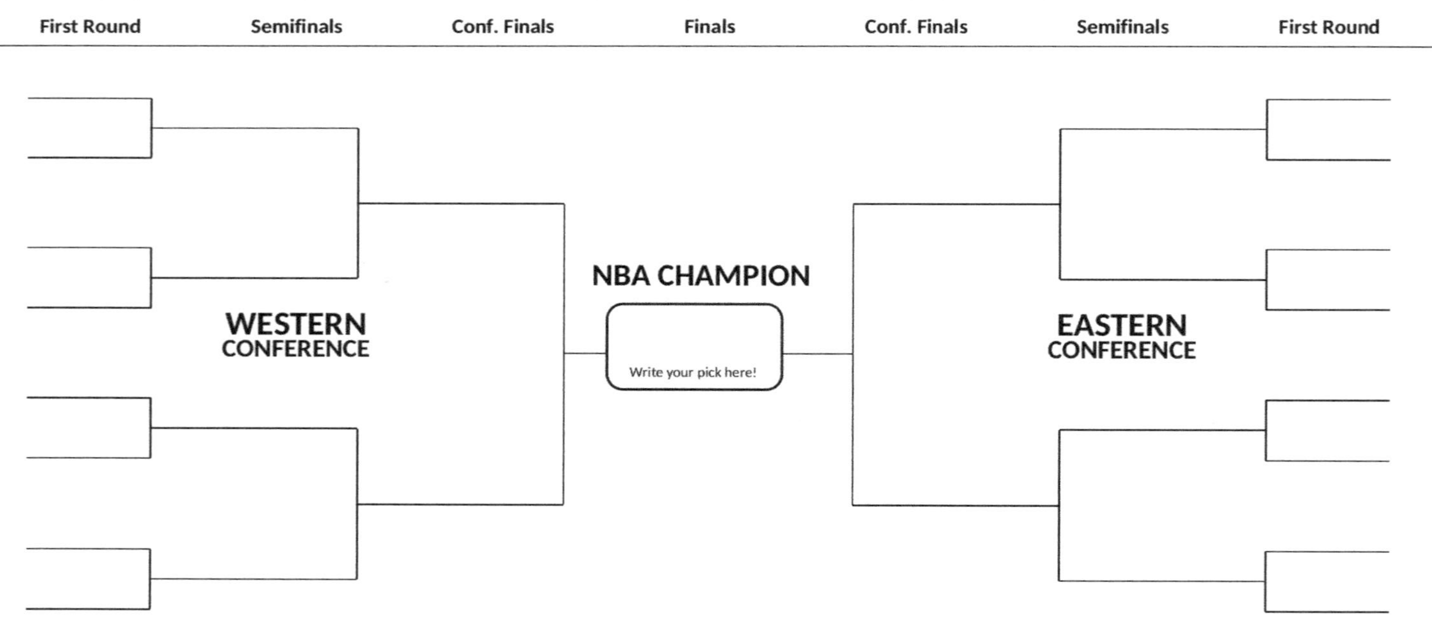

* Fill in your picks and try not to argue with your friends about it!

Part of the Fun Fan Facts: The Unofficial Sports Guide Series

Be the Boss of the Playoffs

You've broken down the matchups. You know which superstar takes over in the fourth quarter. You've seen the bench units that quietly decide series. You've watched the adjustments coaches make when their backs are against the wall.

Now it's time to stop watching and start deciding.

On this page, you are not just a fan. You are the Head Coach drawing up the last play with three seconds left on the clock. You are the GM who built this roster. You are the analyst who saw it all coming.

This is not just filling out a bracket.

This is building your championship run.

Sixteen teams enter the NBA Playoffs. The path is brutal. Best of seven. No shortcuts. No hiding. Every round gets louder, harder, and more personal.

This bracket is your Playoff Control Room.

The Game Plan

1. Survive Round One: Start with the opening round. Which matchup is going seven games? Who has the closer? Who folds under pressure? Make the calls.

2. Feel the Momentum: As you move into the Conference Semifinals and Conference Finals, things change. Role players become heroes. Stars feel the weight. Trust your reads.

3. Own the Finals: Trace your picks all the way to the NBA Finals. When the confetti falls and the trophy is raised, you'll find out who earned it.

House Rules: Circle your boldest upset. That is your official "I knew it" moment.

Choose Your Weapon: Pencil if you want flexibility. Pen if you trust your instincts. Sharpie if you believe in chaos.

Because once the playoffs tip off, there is no rewinding Game 7.

Make your picks. Trust your basketball brain. And let the playoff drama begin.

Fun Facts Wrap-Up

You made it through! You're officially a true superfan! Now it's time to put your knowledge to the test. Share these facts with friends and see who really knows their team best.

Love the series?

Your reviews help other fans discover Fun Fan Facts. If you enjoyed this book, we'd really appreciate you sharing your thoughts and leaving a review.

Want more Fun Fan Facts?

Scan the QR code below to visit our site and explore bonus trivia, challenges, and special extras - including new teams, future series, and collectible fun as they're released.

Collect All the Fun Fan Facts Series!

Check off every book you read. See the full set on Amazon. Search "Fun Fan Facts Jake Liam."

World Cup 2026 Edition

☐ Algeria   ☐ Scotland   ☐ Morocco

☐ France   ☐ Brazil   ☐ Switzerland

☐ Paraguay   ☐ Ivory Coast   ☐ Curaçao

☐ Argentina   ☐ Senegal   ☐ Netherlands

☐ Germany   ☐ Canada   ☐ Tunisia

☐ Portugal   ☐ Japan   ☐ Ecuador

☐ Australia   ☐ South Africa   ☐ New Zealand

☐ Ghana   ☐ Cape Verde   ☐ United States

☐ Qatar   ☐ Jordan   ☐ Egypt

☐ Austria   ☐ South Korea   ☐ Norway

☐ Haiti   ☐ Colombia   ☐ Uruguay

☐ Saudi Arabia   ☐ Mexico   ☐ England

☐ Belgium   ☐ Spain   ☐ Panama

☐ Iran   ☐ Croatia   ☐ Uzbekistan

World Cup 2026 Group Edition

☐ Group A   ☐ Group F   ☐ Group K

☐ Group E   ☐ Group J   ☐ Group D

☐ Group I   ☐ Group C   ☐ Group H

☐ Group B   ☐ Group G   ☐ Group L

English Football Edition

- ☐ Arsenal F.C.
- ☐ Aston Villa F.C.
- ☐ Chelsea F.C.
- ☐ Everton F.C.
- ☐ Fulham F.C.
- ☐ Liverpool F.C.
- ☐ Manchester City
- ☐ Manchester United
- ☐ Newcastle United F.C.
- ☐ Tottenham Hotspur
- ☐ West Ham United
- ☐ Wrexham A.F.C.

NBA Edition

- ☐ Atlanta Hawks
- ☐ Boston Celtics
- ☐ Brooklyn Nets
- ☐ Charlotte Hornets
- ☐ Chicago Bulls
- ☐ Cleveland Cavaliers
- ☐ Dallas Mavericks
- ☐ Denver Nuggets
- ☐ Detroit Pistons
- ☐ Golden State Warriors
- ☐ Houston Rockets
- ☐ Indiana Pacers
- ☐ LA Clippers
- ☐ Los Angeles Lakers
- ☐ Memphis Grizzlies
- ☐ Miami Heat
- ☐ Milwaukee Bucks
- ☐ Minnesota Timberwolves
- ☐ New Orleans Pelicans
- ☐ New York Knicks
- ☐ Oklahoma City Thunder
- ☐ Orlando Magic
- ☐ Philadelphia 76ers
- ☐ Phoenix Suns
- ☐ Portland Trail Blazers
- ☐ Sacramento Kings
- ☐ San Antonio Spurs
- ☐ Toronto Raptors
- ☐ Utah Jazz
- ☐ Washington Wizards

About the Author

Jake is a 13-year-old sports fan who loves football, American football, and basketball. He plays soccer as a goalie and dreams of one day playing for West Ham United and helping teach kids to love the game. His passion for sports runs in the family - his dad was a professional baseball player, and his stepdad sparked his love for West Ham. Through the Fun Fan Facts series, he shares the fun and excitement of sports with fans everywhere.